This Strange Between

Elise Stankus

BookLeaf Publishing
India | USA | UK

elisestankus.com

Presentation by *BookLeaf Publishing*

Web: www.bookleafpub.com

E-mail: info@bookleafpub.com

ISBN: 9789357446884

First edition 2022

DEDICATION

To You

Waking

Suspended here you try to raise your head
Reluctantly you leave this strange between
No monsters lurk beneath your time-worn bed
But echoes lost and shadowed truths unseen
You love this place, and yet you long to leave
You treasure most the secrets you forget
And sleep, like many others, can't retrieve
Your peace behind the burden of regret.
But thoughts begin to clear and plans unfold
Your rise up from the ashes of the night
You find inside yourself some ancient gold
And scars break open skin to let in light
Despite your words, your dreams, and all your
      sins,
The Sun forgives the world; the day begins.

Static

My words are drowning in some distant sea,
A conversation drifts away from me,
My thoughts can't bridge the gap between these
      oceans
Static whispers, mimics, muffles me,
My world used to dance in constant motion
With every step a symbol of devotion
But now we sing, unorchestrated choirs,
Of harsh and wild and unfamiliar notions
I used to hear you whisper through the phone
I used to sit upon a gilded throne
Now patterns dance upon the television
Explaining the difference between lonely and
      alone
Have we lost all semblance of precision?
Has static chased away your sense of vision?
When interruption's louder than my words
My mind is flooded with unmade decisions
The world's falling softly - have you heard?
We are a land of flightless mockingbirds
A silent stillness never screamed so loud
I wake to find the misplaced dream deterred.
Beneath the mist tranquility bows down
Behind a mask expression drops her crown
I seek a spark of soft unhindered clarity

I miss the peace before the awful sound
My words are drowning in some distant sea
A conversation drifts away from me
My thoughts can't bridge the gap between these
        oceans
Static whispers, mimics, muffles me.

Eye Contact

From across the room I see them
A pair of eyes,
And in them, like a mirror,
My own.
Something rushes through my head just then,
A field of purple irises fills my vision to the
      brim
And I overflow.
I sit in a classroom of dark dilated pupils,
Eye contact shocks me - shakes me - into
      waking
It is a connection deeper than the ocean
And as shallow as a reflecting pond.
It holds - holds - holds
Until time is a river we can't cross anymore,
A thing that we can't understand
And the passage of minutes is measured by
      miles
And now your eyes are too far away, and
It breaks,
Not shattering like glass but opening up like
      clouds for rain
My eyes become a river, a saltwater spring,
And I break open, too.

Elevator

Suspended here between these layers of earth
You lean into this ever-strange between
Gravity bows down to weightless worth
And floating upwards, you begin to see
This strange ascent pulls softly on your bones
Pulled upward by a metal puppeteer
Its mouth yawns open with an iron groan
Electric eyes blink to say "we're here!"
Carried by a force we can't control
Despite the friendly buttons on the wall
Feeling so secure, so safe and whole
Until they cut the cables and we fall
But even on those days, we find a way
To float above the day - to elevate.

11:11 AM

I wish.
I wish I could put my wish in words.
I wish I could catch it.
I wish it would stop flying, flaunting, flapping
      wings
I wish I could read the piece of paper wedged in
      its beak.

It won't be my birthday for another seven
      months
But the candles haunt me, taunt me.

I wish the dandelions were in bloom.
I wish to scatter something to the wind.

Perhaps then I would know what it is
That I want.

Perhaps I would know what it is,
How it is,
Why it is,
That I wish.

high ceilings

(i used to) be an astronaut
flight was not a (Dream) but an undisputed
       reality
and i would soar through skies smeared with
       shooting stars,
and hope, one day, to join them.
but now my eyes are small,
and i stand alone (in) high-ceilinged rooms,
feeling as though i am under a microscope
i can't see the (color) on the ceiling anymore.
the walls of the church reach up to Heaven like
      the arms of a child.
(but gravity binds) me here
it's funny how (even) in spaces like (the)se
size seems relative, height irrelevant,
and yet
i still know how little we (Dreamers) are.

Stillness

Fading and flying, cascading and dying
Following falling away
Immobile in motion
Unending devotion
To something that can't be portrayed
Outside the world, the galaxy stills
My reverie dictates my thoughts
An island of violence,
In an ocean of silence,
A life in a world that kills.
But stillness takes me to a realer place
A sea beyond the panic of the day
A spirit of newness
The next world's blueness
Carries me through into grace.

Shadows

My shadow merges softly with another
Amorphous, morphing, slowly, into air
It follows me, an unforgiving other,
A self that casts a shade, a backwards heir
The imprint that the clouds make on the world
Are sentient shadows that precede the rain
Though the earth will shake and skies will swirl,
Prayers offered in the dark are not in vain.

Rain

The world is flooded by drizzle
Slowly, softly filling up, pouring down
I sink in what I cannot live within
I drown in what I cannot live without

The sidewalk lets itself become an ocean
The roof turns to a hand to hold the rain
And me? Behind a window softly blurred,
I swim in something far beyond my words.

The clouds obscure my view of what's above,
My window's a kaleidoscope now
My mind is washed in something thinner than
      water,
A reflective glaze upon my thoughts

My reveries are bluer in the rain,
And gray skies seem to melt the sharpest worlds
Raindrops in every color we can't see
Paint the world, the clouds, the skies, and me

Migraine (Ocean)

There are firecrackers in my head
Waves break upon an unknown shore
(I am the shore, the whispers say)
In and out, in
And out
(I am the shore, I am
The shore)
Waves breaking far below
Cars braking
The ocean taking
Everything from me
(I am the shore, I am
The shore)
It pounds at my thoughts
A tidal tempest pressed against my temples
The storm - no, hurricane -
Rages on, enrages, wrongly
Turns the pages of my mind
(I am the shore, I am
The shore)
Where slowly, softly, vaguely haunting
Firecrackers blaze inside

This Autumn Air

This is autumn air
This kind of space, this slice of time
When you step outside
And the air fills your lungs with gold and dark
      blue
And somehow,
It fills the rest of you, too
This is autumn air
Air that seems a different substance
Than that in the rooms of crowded houses
As though the particles themselves
Are freer, wilder, more than before
Your head feels claustrophobic when under a
      roof
This autumn air is not a roof
But the absence of one,
In the same way "dark" is the absence of "light"
This autumn air is full of light
Heightened by the sharp crisp of leaves
The crunch of a world dying under your feet
Sunlight reflecting off a kaleidoscope of a forest
"Fresh air" is what we call this,
As though it can go stale
As though we can encase autumn air in a plastic
      sleeve

And stamp on it an expiration date
This autumn air is a creature we try to restrain
We try to prolong its stay,
This animal,
This one we love,
This one we fear,
Because this autumn air is wilder than we are,
Conjuring memories we are not ready to
          remember,
It is who we want to be.
I step out into
This autumn air,
And in a breath-
I remember.

Dancing

A song comes on the radio,
Not just a good song,
But a Favorite Song
And something courses through you just then
Something fierce and possessive
And you are moved to madness, the beautiful
      kind
Exploding and sparkling, you ignite
A firecracker smile warms your face
And you remember in a flash
A million other seasons,
A million other moments, movements,
A million other measures,
A million other mountains climbed
Arms and legs move of their own volition, it
      seems
And yet you have never held more control
You let go,
Of moments behind you, and millions more
A million music notes fill you to the core.

Campfire

Watch me dancing,
Alive and entrancing
The fire seems to say
Of kindling commanding
Of skyline demanding
A place that's not burning away

I stand in the fire
That faith will require
And stare into the day
My peace is entire
In spite of the mire
This fire will not fade away.

Driving At Night

We drive through darkness so thick & deep
That you could reach out into the night
And grab a handful
Heavy as lead
And thick as ink
And soft as a panther's coat
Deep as a new ocean
And familiar as an old land
It fills the cracks of broken worlds
It fills you to the core.

Home

I come home after long days, or weeks, or
       maybe months
And sink into cushions
Just a little more softly than last time
Gentle, reserved
Or - maybe - I rip them off the couch
And build them into a castle
With walls reaching up
Far above a moat swirling with chocolate milk

I come home after long days, or weeks, or
       maybe months
And sit in front of the same old television
Nestled beneath blankets older than me
Quiet, simple
Or - maybe - I run outside
Full of the wild
And battle a zillion zigzagging things

I come home after long days, or weeks, or
       maybe months,
And I run my hands over the half-wall,
I play the piano in the blackness of night
I lay under Christmas lights in the middle of
       July,

Or under stars in the middle of December
Or - maybe - I do nothing.

What is home if not the places you can transcend
        reality?
Who is family if not the people you transcend it
        with?
I come home after long days, or weeks, or
        maybe months
And I find no time has passed at all.

after long days

after long days
we sink into blankets
that remind us of who we used to be
our cradles and cribs still haunt us,

after long days
we return to ourselves
under blankets that weigh down our fears
pressed into the soft crisp of new sheets
we dissolve
into
ourselves.

We Are Untitled

At the end of the day
We are unnamed masterpieces
But our author isn't finished.

I let my world bleed into the bigger one,
I let my words begin a new beginning

Suspended here I try to raise my head,
Suspended among flightless mockingbirds
Suspended at the end of endless days
Despite the names suspended here in us
Suspended here we are still untitled

I let my world bleed into a bigger one
I let my words begin a new beginning

This Strange Between

Falling into sleep
And instead of your heart
Your head is heavy,
Pressed against the pillow
Slowly silently your eyes sweep
Closed.
The silence is sweet
The stillness soft
The pillow dark and comforting beneath your
       head

Daytime gives us strange illusions
We were the reckless
We were the wild
We asked of the world what we couldn't give
But here in the darkness,
Here in the silent stillness
We are ourselves

We are the ones who straddle these worlds
Paradise hovers outside our reach,
And we sit - somewhat impatiently -

In anticipation of what comes next
And we are the ones who wait.
The ones who live to tell our own tales
We are the ones of the stories
We, with our simple lives and monotonous tunes
We live in many worlds,
With our pain,
With our ever-pouring rain
We with our joy, our toys, our ploys
We are the beautiful ones, I think.
We are not the authors who sit up late at night
        laboring over lives not their own
We are the stories told.
We are the clouds with gilded gleam,
At the end of the day,
We are this strange between

ACKNOWLEDGEMENT

Before I begin, I want to thank you, the reader, for taking this journey with me. Whether or not you are aware, you have accompanied me through the ups and downs of writing and publishing a poetry collection, and I am grateful for your support of my writing.

First, I have to thank my family for their constant encouragement of my ever-present writing projects. I am so thankful for all of you, and I hope you know that many of the poems in this collection were inspired by you.

Thank you to Gabby and Bianca, for your friendship. I'm glad I didn't have to do this alone, and I wish you the best of luck.

Thank you to everyone who read If We Fall In The Forest. Thanks for coming back.

Thank you to all the poets who have inspired me throughout the years. You know who you are.

To God, for giving me a gift and an opportunity I am forever grateful for.

See you in the next book!

Love, Elise